All THINGS WOLVES For Kids

FILLED WITH PLENTY OF FACTS, PHOTOS, AND FUN TO LEARN ALL ABOUT WOLVES

ANIMAL READS

THIS BOOK BELONGS TO...

_____

_____

WWW.ANIMALREADS.COM

FOLLOW THE PAW PRINTS

Get Ready to Run Wild with Wolves! 1

What is a Wolf? 5

The Wolf Family Album — 11
   Meet the Pack!

Built for Adventure — 35
   A Wolf's Amazing Features

The Pack — Better Together 49

Wild Places — Where Wolves Roam 55

What's for Dinner? — 65
   A Wolf's Favorite Foods

Growing Up Wolf — 71
   From Pup to Pack Member

Well Done, Wolf Expert! 85

Thank You! 89

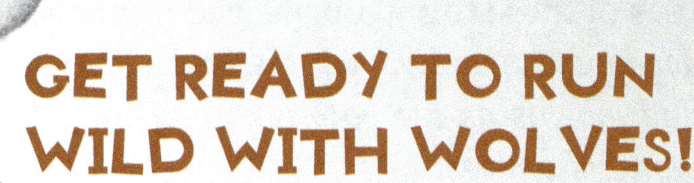

GET READY TO RUN WILD WITH WOLVES!

Ahwoooooooooo, there, fellow wolf enthusiast! Are you keen to put on your detective hat and head into the wilderness to sniff out all there is to know about wolves?

Then you're in luck!

In this book, we will explore every aspect of this majestic animal, from the tip of its twitchy nose to the end of its fluffy tail. We'll meet different types of wolves — *some with fur as white as snow and others with coats as gray as a stormy sky*. We'll find out what these hungry hunters love to munch on and whether they prefer to live alone or with their families.

Along our journey into the wild, we promise we'll have a howling good time discovering the secret lives of these furry, four-legged animals. *So why don't you lace up your hiking boots, let out your best ahwooooo, and join us as we paw our way into the wonderful world of wolves?*

Let's embark on a wild adventure, one page at a time, through some of the world's most incredible landscapes. Keep your eyes peeled, your ears perked up, and your mind ready to soak up all the wolf-tastic facts!

Let's jump right in!

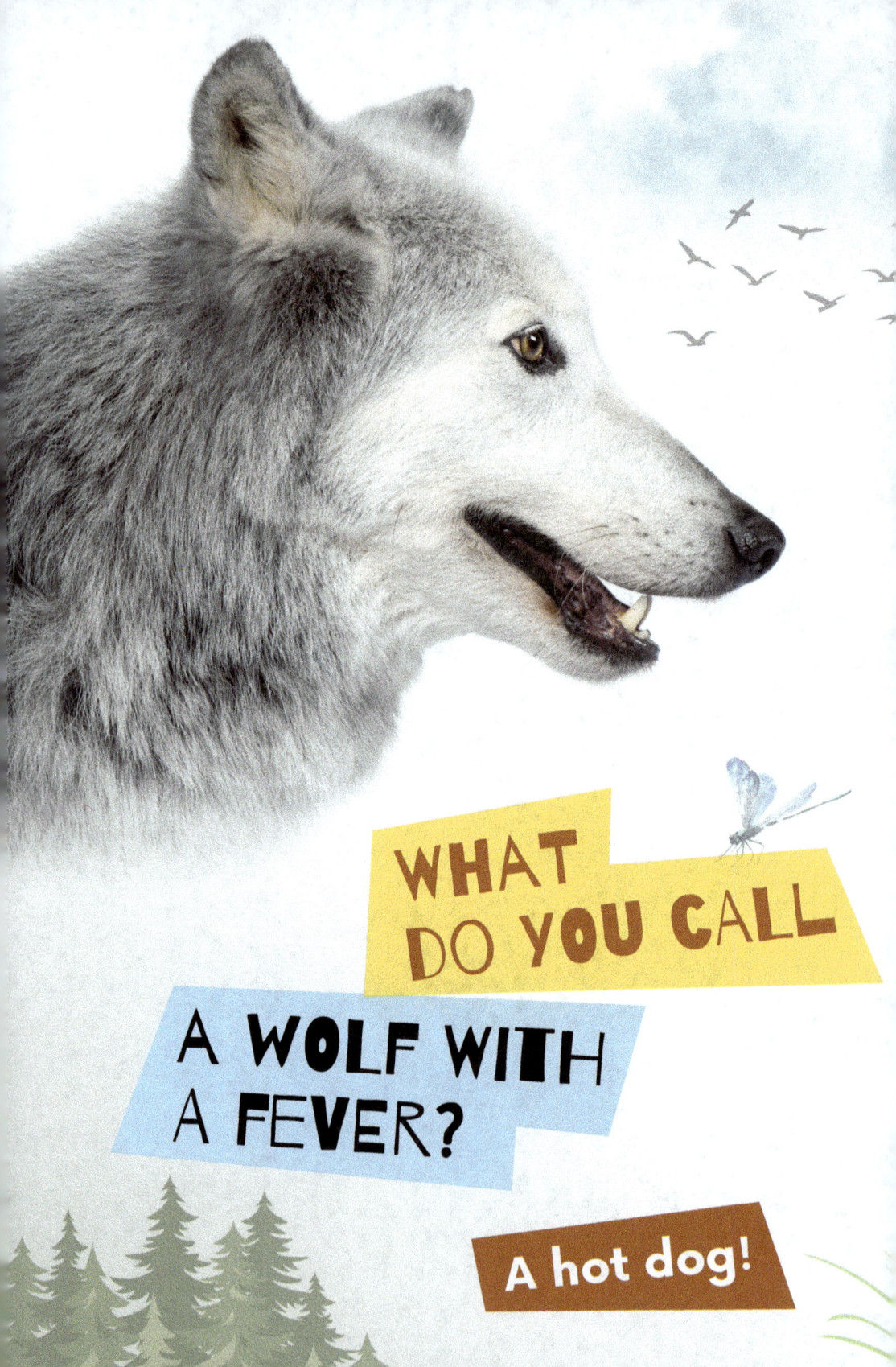

WHAT IS A WOLF?

Wolves are part of a particular group of animals called **mammals**. Mammals have warm blood pumping through their hearts, grow hair or fur, breathe fresh air into their lungs, and the mommies feed their little ones with milk. As you may have guessed, humans are also mammals because we share all these traits as well.

But this is where the similarities between humans and wolves end. Because, you see, wolves aren't just *any* kind of mammals — they're part of a fantastic club known as the **Canidae family**. This animal family includes foxes, jackals, coyotes, and dogs — yes, the kind of dog you might have as a pet! If you have a small breed of dog, like a chihuahua, you may wonder if they are also related to wolves. And YES, they are! They may look very different, but remember that dogs have changed a lot over the last few hundred years. Most modern dog breeds might not resemble wolves anymore. Still, they have all come from the same **ancestor** — which means that a chihuahua and a wild wolf might share the same **great-great-great-great-great-great-(a great many times over)-Grandpa.**

Pretty crazy thought, right?

Much like human families, which are groups of people closely related to one another, animal families are also groups of related animals. In the *Canidae family*, we find animals that walk on all fours, have sharp teeth, a long snout, pointy ears, and a fantastic sense of smell. Of all the members of this huge family, wolves are the largest.

The term "family" is a word that scientists like to use when they talk about animal groups. Think of it like sorting your toy boxes — *you might put trucks with cars, stuffed bears with stuffed dogs, and small building blocks with big building blocks, right?* Scientists do the same with animals, sorting them into groups that share similarities so they can learn more about them and see how they all fit together in the giant puzzle of nature.

Grouping similar animals helps us understand who's who in the animal kingdom. It also tells us which animals are like distant relatives and which are like really close siblings. For example, wolves and dogs are more like siblings, but wolves and foxes are more like third-degree cousins!

Did you know?

Wolves can sprint much faster than the fastest humans on Earth. While the speediest humans can run up to 28 miles per hour, a wolf can zip through the forest at a whopping 35 miles per hour! Imagine trying to win a race against that speedy furball?!

HOWL
ABOUT THAT!

THE WOLF FAMILY ALBUM —
MEET THE PACK!

If you know *anything* about dogs, you know that there are maaany different breeds. It might be pretty wacky to think that a pug is closely related to a Great Dane, but hey...the animal world is crazy like that!

In the same way, there are also different species of wolves, each with unique traits and talents. Much like dogs, not every wolf is created equal — some like to chill out in the freezing snow, while others prefer warmer temperatures and frolicking in fields full of flowers. Some are big and strong, and others are smaller and more agile.

Let's dive a little deeper and get up close (*but not too close!*) to five amazing wolf species: **the Gray, Arctic, Red, Ethiopian,** and **Mexican wolves.** Each of these wolves is a furry celebrity in its own right, with unique traits that make them incredibly special.

ANIMAL READS

GRAY WOLVES

Consider these the **BIG bosses of the wolf world.** They boast some pretty impressive stats that make them stand out, *literally!*

First off, let's talk size. Gray wolves are like the basketball players of the wolf family—they're tall and have long and powerful legs that make them **great at running and jumping.** They are particularly good at long-distance running and can easily cover about 12 miles (19 km) in a single day. When

sprinting over short distances, a gray wolf can reach speeds of 40 miles an hour (64 km/hr) — that's faster than you're allowed to drive in most city neighborhoods!

Don't let the name 'Gray wolf' fool you! These amazing animals can wear many different colors — gray, brown, cream, reddish, and even black like these two wolves. Some even mix and match colors, like wearing a patchwork coat!

Gray wolves can be as long as a family-size kitchen table, with some adults measuring an impressive 6.5 feet (2 meters) from the tip of their nose to the end of their tail. Standing at about 2.5-3 feet (75-90 cm) tall at their shoulder, they're about the same size as a Great Dane — but much fiercer and built for hunting in the wild!

Did you know?

Wolves have been around for a very long time — almost a million years! The gray wolf, the kind we see today, evolved around 300,000 years ago. That's way before people started taming wolves to become dogs!

Now, where can you find these magnificent creatures?

Gray wolves are experienced world travelers! In fact, they have been found in North America, Europe, and Asia, so they're pretty good at making themselves at home anywhere, whether in a chilly forest, a grassy meadow, or even a dry desert.

One of the most incredible traits of gray wolves is their howl, **the loudest of all wolf species.** A gray wolf's howl can reach volumes of up to 110 decibels, which is about the loudness of a chainsaw or a rock concert! Howling for wolves is not just for fun but used, much like human voices, to communicate with one another. Amazingly, each wolf has a unique howl, allowing members of a pack to easily recognize one another even across great distances. A wolf's howl can be heard up to 10 miles (16km) away! Wolves howl to say "hello" or to warn other wolves to keep out of their territory. Howling is just one part of a wolf's secret language. They also bark and whine, with every sound carrying a different meaning.

Gray wolves are **amazing team players!** Like a close-knit family, they live together in groups called **packs**. These packs can have up to 15 wolves

ALL THINGS WOLVES FOR KIDS // 17

or more, and they do everything as a team — from hunting dinner to playing together in the forest. Each wolf has its own special job that helps keep the whole pack strong and healthy.

Did you know?

Scientists used to think each pack had a single boss — an **alpha male** who made all the decisions. But in the last twenty years, they discovered something different. Wolf packs are actually led by both parents working together as a team. These mother and father wolves (called the **alpha pair**) have pups and guide the whole pack through teamwork.

ARCTIC WOLVES

Now might be a good time to put on a really warm jacket because we are heading to the far north of our planet to the frosty world of the Arctic wolf.

Known as the **kings and queens of the ice**, Arctic wolves are **among the toughest wolves** of all. They live in unforgiving conditions and have developed some nifty tricks to survive in one of the coldest places on Earth!

Arctic wolves are **the second-largest species**, slightly smaller than gray wolves. They can be between 3 to 6 feet (up to 1.8m) in length and stand to about 28 inches at the shoulders, or 70 cm. They're about the size of a Siberian Husky — which makes sense since both are built for life in the snow!

Nature has given Arctic wolves the perfect outfit for their icy home — a thick, white coat that never comes off! This gorgeous fur doesn't just keep them toasty warm; it also helps them blend right into their snowy world. They share this frozen kingdom with polar bears, living in a place so cold that barely any trees can grow. Imagine a world of endless snow and ice — that's where Arctic wolves call home!

Where is the Arctic?

The Arctic is a super interesting and special place at the top of our world, filled with cool animals and icy landscapes! Imagine looking at a globe or a map — can you find the North Pole? The Arctic is all of the white area around it. Canada, the USA, Greenland, Russia, Iceland, Norway, Finland, and Sweden all have parts of their land in the Arctic. However, the Arctic wolf does not live in every country in the Arctic region, and it is only found in the USA, Canada, and Greenland!

One of the most unique things about Arctic Wolves is their **color**. Their fur is as white as the snowy landscapes in which they live, which makes them really good at a game of hide and seek. This white fur helps them blend in — or **camouflage** — with their frosty surroundings so they can sneak up on their dinner without being spotted.

These fluffy wolves blend right into their snowy world!

But it's not just their fur that makes Arctic wolves special. Their **ears and noses are smaller** than those of other wolf species, which is a smart way they adapted to maintain body warmth — it helps them save heat and stay toasty in the freezing cold!

Arctic Wolves are indeed super tough. They don't mind the cold and are used to traveling long distances to find food. They can walk over 30 miles (48 km) every day looking for a tasty meal.

RED WOLVES

Brrrrr, it's been rather cold exploring the Arctic region, right? Let's defrost a little and explore the warmer forests of North America. Maybe, if we get really lucky, we might catch a glimpse of the beautiful red wolf.

Red Wolves are **medium-sized members** of the wolf family, neither too big nor too small. They're

 ALL THINGS WOLVES FOR KIDS // 23

about as long as an adult human is tall, so imagine your mom or dad lying down, and you've got the length of a red wolf from nose to tail tip — about 5,5 feet or 1.70 meters!

These copper-colored adventurers used to roam all over the southeastern United States, but nowadays, they're mostly found in just a few places, like the wild and beautiful lands of North Carolina. They love swamps, forests, and prairies, where they can successfully hide from and hunt other animals.

You would have to agree that one of the most striking things about the red wolf is its **stunning fur,** which is a mix of reddish-brown, tan, and black. It's like they've been painted with the colors of a sunset, making them one of the most beautiful wolves you'll ever see!

But being beautiful isn't the red wolf's *only* claim to fame. These wolves are super **family-oriented** and like to stick with their pack, which is usually smaller than the gray wolf's. The red wolf pack normally has only five to eight members — a small, united family that hunts, plays, and howls together.

Two red wolves cuddle up in the snow.

Did you know?

Sadly, red wolves are some of the rarest wolves on the planet and are considered **endangered**. *This is when an animal species decreases in number for various reasons. Usually, it's because their wilderness homes are destroyed by natural disasters or human activity. Luckily, a great bunch of really smart and caring people are working hard to help them recover. By protecting their homes and helping them raise their adorable pups, we hope to see more of these sunset hunters.*

ETHIOPIAN WOLVES

The highlanders of the wolf world, the Ethiopian wolf lives high on Africa's roof, where the air is crisp and the views are spectacular!

Ethiopian wolves are very slender, with long legs that make them look like they're always ready to run a marathon. They're about as tall as a big bicycle, and when they stand on their tiptoes, they can peek over your dining table! From nose to tail, they can be from 3 to 3.5 feet (around 1 meter) in length.

You'll find these majestic creatures **only in Ethiopia**, a gorgeous country in Africa that is famous for its luscious green plains and high mountains. Their favorite spots are way up high, where they can gaze out over their kingdom of grass and rock. From these heights, they can easily spot both their next meal and any dangers that might be sneaking up on them.

Ethiopian wolves have a **fiery red coat with white markings and a black, bushy tail.** They look like they've been dipped in a paint pot of bold and beautiful colors. Given their slender body and burnt-orange coat, the Ethiopian wolf is often mistaken for a fox — but it is indeed a very special species of wolf! Unlike most other wolf species, this Ethiopian treasure prefers to live in small packs — usually only comprising an alpha pair and their immediate pups. A very tight-knit family unit!

Sadly, just like the Red Wolf, the Ethiopian Wolf is also super rare. They're the most **endangered** African carnivores, which means we've got to cheer them on and help protect their mountain homes. By keeping their environment safe and sound, we can help these mountain monarchs continue to rule their rocky realms.

MEXICAN WOLVES

Feeling in the mood to explore some more of the world's remotest corners? Let's bid goodbye to Africa and venture into the sun-scorched deserts of North America to meet a really hardy animal: the Mexican wolf!

Mexican wolves might be **the smallest of the North American wolves**, but don't let their size

fool you—**they're as tough as cacti!** They're about as long as a teenager is tall when they stretch from their nose to their tail (4.5-5.5 feet, or 1.5m) and stand about 2 feet (60 cm) tall. That's similar to the size of a German Shepherd!

These desert dynamos live in the southwestern United States and Mexico, roaming through **scrublands and forests**. They're the cowboys of the wolf world, loving the wide-open spaces where they can chase after adventures under the vast, starry sky.

One of their unique features is their beautiful fur, a **patchwork quilt of gray, rust, and cream**. It's like they've been sprinkled with the colors of the desert—dusty grays of the sagebrush, rusty reds of the rocks, and creamy whites of the bleached bones scattered in the sand!

The Mexican wolf, known as *"El Lobo"* in Spanish, is a real social butterfly, living in close-knit packs that work together to raise their pups and hunt for meals. Their wolf packs typically consist of about 4 to 8 individuals (*similar to the red wolves*). They are **highly territorial**, so they fiercely defend their homes from predators like mountain lions, coyotes, and other wolf packs wanting to compete for land.

The Mexican wolves' journey hasn't been all sunny days. This distinguished creature almost went **extinct**, coming close to disappearing altogether. Luckily, many dedicated humans stepped in to give these wolves a helping hand, reintroducing them to the wild and watching over them as they make their comeback. *Phew!*

A red wolf stops for a drink from a stream.

BUILT FOR ADVENTURE —
A WOLF'S AMAZING FEATURES

Wolves are fascinating creatures with some truly amazing features that allow them to live in the wild. *Everything* about their bodies has evolved to help them survive in their often unfriendly environment.

Let's start by looking closely at their coats and fur!

FUR-OCIOUS COATS

Imagine **having a coat that changes with the weather** — *how cool would that be?* Well, wolves boast that kind of magical coat.

When the world looks like a giant snow globe in winter, **wolves grow super thick and fluffy fur.** This is like wearing the warmest winter jacket ever. This winter fur has many layers, including a fuzzy undercoat that traps warm air close to the skin — think of it as nature's thermal underwear!

But wolves can't wear their winter coats all year; they'd get too hot when the sun starts to sizzle. So, as the snow melts and the flowers poke their heads out, wolves shed their heavy fur coat, much like you might take off your own heavy coat once spring begins. This shedding reveals a **sleeker, lighter summer coat** underneath, perfect for staying cool when the forest turns into a leafy sunroom.

You might wonder, *"How does a wolf's fur know when to change?"* Well, it's all thanks to the daylight. As the days get longer or shorter, wolves' bodies

get the hint that it's time to switch up their wardrobe. It's as if their fur has its own calendar and clock, telling them when it's time to dress for snowball fights or undress for sunny picnics.

And here's a fun fact: **wolf fur isn't just one color all over.** It's a mix of blacks, grays, browns, and whites that blend together. This mix helps them blend into the trees and rocks, making them hide-and-seek champions of the wild.

Lastly, wolf coats also feature a **waterproof layer.** That's right, wolves have built-in raincoats to stay dry and warm during unpleasant weather!

FANG-TASTIC TEETH

Want to know what makes a wolf's mouth so special? Just like you have different teeth for biting and chewing, wolves have a fantastic set of teeth that work together like the perfect hunting toolkit. Let's discover what each type of tooth can do!

First, we have the **incisors**, *the little teeth at the front*. Wolves use these like forks to nibble off tiny pieces of food. They're perfect for the "tidy eating" part of the meal.

Next up are the long and pointy **canines** that look like icicles. These are the famous fangs we hear about in stories. Wolves use their fangs to grab onto something and hold it super tight. These teeth are incredibly powerful and can even crush bones!

Now, let's peek at the **premolars** and **molars**, the big, flat teeth at the back of the mouth. These are like the wolf's kitchen knives. They chop and slice the meat into bite-sized pieces that are easy to swallow.

All these teeth don't just help wolves eat; they also keep them healthy. Chewing on bones cleans their teeth — like brushing, so they can keep their fang-tastic smiles looking good all year round!

PAW-SOME FOOTWEAR

Wolves' paws are better than the most incredible hiking boots ever designed. They're built to handle long treks through forests, over mountains, and across frozen streams. Each paw has four toes up front, each with its own claw, like built-in cleats for extra grip when sprinting to catch dinner or playing tag with their wolf pals.

But it's not just the claws that make these paws special. The bottom of a wolf's paw has a soft pad,

like a squishy cushion, that helps them move quietly. This is super handy when sneaking up on something they want to surprise.

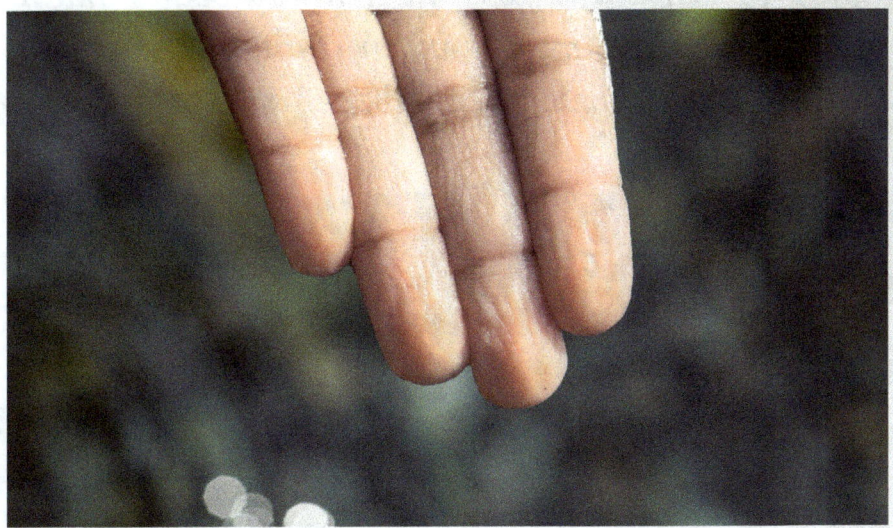

Have you ever noticed how your fingers get wrinkly when you soak in the tub or go swimming? Well, wolves have something similar on their paws. It's called "**paw pad texture**," and it helps them not to slip and slide on wet or icy ground. So even when it's slipperier than a banana peel, wolves can keep their cool and stay firmly on their feet.

When winter comes, and parts of the world get covered in snow, wolves can adapt. Their paws spread out to make a bigger footprint, which keeps them from sinking into the snow. You can think of it like having snowshoes that help them float on top of the snow instead of sinking right into it!

Did you know?

Wolves' back paws are bigger than their front paws. Why? To help them carry their heavy bodies and to help them not to tip over when running or stopping quickly. It helps them balance better and run faster!

SNIFF-TASTIC SNOUTS

Wolves have super-duper sniffers that could win a gold medal in the *Smelling Olympics*. They **can smell things that are very far away**, even farther than your school bus ride home! As you can im-

agine, this is very useful while hunting. *You can probably smell it when dinner is getting cooked in the oven over in the kitchen, but a wolf can smell it when it's being cooked in the next neighborhood!*

And that's not all! Wolves' noses are also great for making friends and saying "hello." They use their sense of smell to figure out who's who in the wolf world. Each wolf has its own particular smell, like how everyone has their own look. When a wolf takes a big sniff, it's like reading a story about where the other wolf has been and what it's been up to.

Now, imagine if you could smell your way home? Well, wolves can do just that! Their noses help

them remember the smell of their home turf so they can wander far and wide and still find their way back.

Wolf's noses are also crucial for talking without making a sound. When wolves leave little **pee-mails** (*yes, pee-mails!*) on trees and rocks, they're leaving messages for other wolves. They can signal messages like, "*I was here, this is my spot!*" or "*Hey, I'm looking for a friend!*" You may have seen dogs do something similar as they walk around the park.

Did you know?

Wolves have a particular part of their nose called **the Jacobson's organ** *that helps them smell even better. It's especially handy when a wolf wants to find a friend or avoid bumping into a grumpy bear.*

TAIL(OR) MADE

A wolf's tail isn't just for wagging when it's happy — it's one of their most impressive tools, used for everything from talking to staying warm!

First off, a wolf's tail is like a big, fluffy **flag** that they wave around to talk to their wolf buddies. When a wolf holds its tail high, it's saying, "*Look at me, I'm the boss!*" And when it tucks its tail down

low, it's like saying, "*Oops, my bad,*" or "*I'm just chilling, and I mean no harm.*" It's their way of giving signals, a secret code, that they can use without making a single sound.

When the weather turns *chilly-willy* cold, wolves have a clever trick. They can curl up into a furry

ball and wrap their tails around their noses like a cozy scarf. This helps keep their faces warm in the most bitter winter weather!

That's not all, though, wolves also use their tails to help them balance, just like tightrope walkers use long poles! Whether they're climbing over rocky mountain paths or leaping after prey, their tail helps keep them steady and stops them from falling over.

Did you know?

When wolves trek through deep snow, their tails help them leave a trail. Other wolves can follow this trail like breadcrumbs, so nobody gets lost!

THE PACK — BETTER TOGETHER

You may have already heard that wolves are *"pack animals"* — this is because wolves live in... well, **packs!** Wolf packs can range in size depending on the species. Most wolf packs have about six or seven members, but some can have more, especially if there's plenty of food around.

Each wolf in the pack has a unique role, kind of like how in your family, someone might be the cook, someone else the fixer-upper, and someone else the storyteller or the one who takes the rubbish out once a week.

Remember how we learned that wolf packs don't only have one male boss? That's right! They have what is known as an **alpha pair** that leads the pack. They're like the mom and dad of the family, the ones that make the big decisions, like where to go for dinner (*which is called 'hunting' in wolf language*) and where to travel. The alpha male and alpha female are the parents of most of the pups in the pack.

Next are the **beta wolves**, who are like the second-in-command or vice presidents of the pack! The beta wolves will help during hunts and with the raising of the pups and generally just help out the alpha pair in their wolfy business. They are the aunts and uncles of the babies of the pack!

Then, a wolf pack has the **hunters**. These wolves are super good at chasing and catching dinner and this is their primary job — to provide food for the pack. They work together like a soccer team, each playing their part to make sure everyone in the pack gets to eat.

Some packs, especially the big ones, have a wolf called an **omega**. This wolf is a bit like the class clown, helping to keep things fun and light in the pack. Even though the omega might be at the bottom of the wolfy ladder, they're still loved and play an essential part in keeping harmony in the family.

Did you know?

Alpha, beta, and omega are letters of the Greek alphabet — they're actually the first, second, and last letters of the alphabet. They are often used to mean the first (or best), the second in command, and even the last of the group. Even the word "alphabet" comes from the Greek words "alpha" and "beta!"

The remainder of a wolf pack is usually made up of other adult wolves, teenagers, and pups, many of them older offspring of the alpha pair. Everyone helps out with different tasks, like taking care of the pups, watching out for danger, and even playing with each other to learn necessary wolf skills.

Like in your family, where everyone has chores and helps each other, every wolf has a job to do in a pack. All the wolves work together to ensure the pack stays happy and healthy!

WHAT'S THE NAME FOR THE ENTRANCE TO A WOLF'S DEN?

A HOWL-way!

WILD PLACES — WHERE WOLVES ROAM

Wolves have unique places where they love to live, play, and snooze. These places are called **habitats**, meaning the areas where wolves can be found. These adaptable animals have a knack for making themselves at home in various places, from the icy, snowy landscapes of the Arctic to the scorching hot plains of the North American desert and in the luscious mountain forests in Ethiopia.

Let's explore some of these habitats now.

FORESTS

Wolves love living in forests because the trees keep them hidden, and they can sneak up on anything they want to hunt. Forests also house most animals wolves like to eat, like deer and rabbits. The forest floor is covered with soft leaves, moss, and dirt, so it is like walking on a carpet — soft, comfy, and super quiet. Wolves can tiptoe around without making a sound, just like when you're trying to sneak up and scare someone!

The forest is also like a giant umbrella made of leaves. When it rains, the trees help keep the wolves dry. And when it's super sunny and hot, the forest offers shady spots to lie down and nap.

MOUNTAINS

Living high up in the mountains is also great, as wolves have many places to hide. Different caves and holes allow them to hide, rest, and hunt. Wolves are great climbers and have fantastic balance, so climbing steep slopes is no problem!

Atop a mountain also allows wolves to see for miles and miles, helping them spot their next meal or keeping an eye out for a predator that might be hunting *them*. It's like sitting at the top of a slide and seeing the whole playground.

The air up in the mountains is also typically cooler, so even when it's hot down below, wolves can chill out in their natural air conditioning. And the mountains have many little streams and springs with fresh water for wolves to drink.

DESERTS

Okay, let's talk about dry and sunny deserts and why wolves think it's a neat place to hang out! Deserts can be really hot, but wolves are clever and know how to stay cool. They find secret places to rest during the day, like a shady cave or a spot under a big rock. Even though the desert has few trees or lakes, wolves can still find water hidden in the ground or saved up in plants.

And guess what? At night, the desert can get pretty chilly. Wolves have thick fur that keeps them just right — *not too hot, not too cold* — so they can run around at night when it's much cooler.

The desert is also a quiet place where wolves can hear really well. With their super-duper hearing, they can listen for a little mouse scrambling about or a friend calling from afar.

ICE AND SNOW OF THE ARCTIC

As we have learned, a species of wolf thrives in the ice and snow of the Arctic — **the Arctic wolf,**

of course! With their super fluffy white fur to keep them warm and their double-strong sense of smell, Arctic wolves are excellent at finding food, even when it seems like there's nothing there. They can sniff out where animals are hiding under the snow!

These wolves have perfectly adapted to rough conditions and can even sleep directly in the cold ice. There is no need to search for a cave or a den. They dig a little hole in the snow, curl up, and use their fluffy tails as a warm, fuzzy blanket over their noses. Plus, wolves can see far away since there aren't many trees or other places to hide in the Arctic. This helps them keep an eye out for their family and make sure everyone is safe.

PRAIRIES

Wide-open grasslands are paw-sitively perfect habitats for wolves. Prairies are full of tall grasses and wildflowers, which creates the perfect hunting grounds. Plenty of areas to hide in allow wolves to sneak up on prey, like bunnies and deer. Wolves also dig cozy dens in the prairie ground, where they snuggle up for naps and care for their adorable wolf pups.

HOW DO WOLVES EAT THEIR FOOD?

They WOLF it down!

WHAT'S FOR DINNER?
A WOLF'S FAVORITE FOODS

Wolves are not picky eaters, but they mainly eat one thing... **meat**! This means they are what are called **carnivores**. These animals primarily love to eat meat, just like lions, tigers, and even your little kitty at home.

Being a carnivore is pretty cool because it means you're part of a group of animals with super skills for finding and eating other animals. Wolves have pointy teeth for tearing, strong jaws for chomping, and speedy legs for chasing.

The main dish on a wolf's menu often includes animals with hooves — think deer prancing in the forest or elk chilling by the river. But wolves don't always eat big meals. Sometimes, they snack on smaller critters, like rabbits or squirrels.

And here's a shocker — **wolves sometimes eat berries and fruits!** Yep, even these meat lovers enjoy some fresh blueberries or a crunchy apple every now and then. Berries and fruits are like nature's vitamins, packed with good stuff that helps wolves stay healthy and strong. These sweet treats give wolves nutrients they cannot get from meat alone. Berries are also full of water, which is essential for wolves, especially in places where water is harder to find, like the desert.

Another reason wolves might munch on berries is that sometimes the meat can be tricky to catch. Wolves can get a bit hungry when the deer are extra sneaky or the rabbits run off like speed demons.

So, they'll snack on berries and fruits to fill their tummies until they can catch their next meal.

HUNTING STRATEGIES

Wolves have some cool tricks and strategies up their furry sleeves to catch their dinner. They love to work together, and each wolf has an important job. Some wolves chase the animals they're trying to catch over a long distance, while others sneak around to surprise them.

It's really important that they work as a team since the animals they like to hunt, like deer and elk, are usually much bigger than they are. It would be hard for a lone wolf to successfully hunt a fully grown elk. **Only as a team do they stand a chance!**

Wolves commonly circle their prey, spreading out and surrounding the animal so it has nowhere

to run. Sometimes, wolves use the waiting game: they find a good spot near a trail where animals come to drink water or munch on grass. Then, they quietly sit and wait. When an animal comes by, the wolves are ready to jump out and hopefully have a successful catch.

Wolves will always try to eat A LOT after a triumphant hunt. Although they are excellent hunters, food can be hard to find. So, their stomachs are built to handle going without food for up to two weeks if needed! Although they don't prefer this, it is a way to survive. It makes sense, then, that when they finally have a meal in front of them, they make sure to eat as much as possible — sometimes up to 20 pounds of meat in one meal!

WHAT IS A WOLF'S FAVORITE TIME OF YEAR?

The HOWL-o-days!

GROWING UP WOLF —
FROM PUP TO PACK MEMBER

Did you know that a wolf pup cannot see or hear anything when it is born? *Imagine that!* If you have ever met a newborn puppy or even a kitten, you will know that many animals cannot see or hear when they are first born.

Wolves go through extraordinary changes from the time they are born, tiny, deaf, and blind, to a time when they are fully grown and ready to start a family of their own and maybe even become a part of a pack's alpha pair.

Let's take a look at the life cycle of this enchanting animal!

WOLF PUPS

In the cozy corners of the wilderness, tucked away in dens, something magical happens. *Wolf pups are born!* But they don't come into the world one at

This young wolf pup, probably around 3-4 weeks old, takes its first adventures outside the den.

a time; they arrive with many brothers and sisters. They're all part of what we call a '**litter**,' which is a fancy way of saying a group of baby animals that are born at the same time to the same mom.

Usually, a wolf mom will have about **four to six** pups in a litter, but sometimes there can be even

more. *That's a lot of wolfy babies!* When they're born, wolf pups are super tiny and can't see or hear, but that doesn't stop them from making A LOT of noise! They let out little howls and whimpers to talk to their mom, brothers, and sisters.

For the first two weeks, wolf pups are living in a dark world — not only are they blind, but they are also safely tucked into a dark and hidden den. Amazingly, even without sight and sound, they know how to snuggle up to their mom for some warm, yummy milk. This special milk from their mom gives them all the nutrients they need to start growing strong.

As the days go by, something astonishing happens. Their eyes open, and they get their first blurry look at the outside world. It's like when you first wake up in the morning; everything's a little fuzzy until you rub your eyes. Their ears start to work, too, and they can hear sounds for the first time.

With their eyes and ears open, the world becomes an exciting place full of things to see, hear, and sniff. But these pups don't just jump up and start running around. Oh no, they're still a bit wobbly and must learn to walk without tumbling over their paws. It's like riding a bike for the first time — it takes some practice! They wobble, waddle, and yes, they tumble!

As they practice, they get better and better, and soon, they're not just walking; they're running and playing games with their **littermates.** A "littermate" is a fancy word for a brother or sister from the same litter. They chase each other's tails, pounce, and play fight. It might look like they're just having fun, but they're actually learning important skills, like how to be strong and talk to each other using body language.

The wolf pups are also learning how to work together and what it means to be gentle or firm. They're also figuring out who is the most daring, the sneakiest, and the fastest of the litter.

TEENAGE WOLVES

When wolf pups are about six months old, they hit their "*teenage*" years. That's when they become like middle schoolers of the wolf world — full of energy and ready to test their limits. They're not little pups anymore, but they're also not grownups just yet. They're in that in-between stage where every day is a new chance to **learn and explore.**

These teen wolves are on the prowl and have a lot to prove. They're getting bigger, bolder, and braver every day and want everyone to know. Their legs

are longer, their paws are bigger, and their howls start sounding like grown-ups!

The young wolves now begin to tag along on hunting trips with the adults, similar to apprentices learning a trade—watching, listening, and practicing the skills they need to survive in the wild. They're not doing the actual hunting yet, but they're paying close attention to the grown-up wolves' every move.

The pack is patient with these teenage wolves, even when they make mistakes. Remember learning to tie your shoes or ride a bike? Sometimes, you get it all wrong before you get it right. The teen wolves might get too excited and scare away the prey, or they might play when they should be quiet. *But that's all part of growing up wolf!*

This is also when teen wolves start finding their place in the pack. Just like you might find out you're really good at math, drawing, or soccer, teen wolves discover what they're best at. Some might be great at leading a chase, while others might be excellent at sniffing out trails or keeping an eye on their younger siblings.

The pack's territory becomes their playground and classroom. They learn the best places to find food, where to drink, and where to rest. They also learn the *"wolf rules"*—like how to communicate with howls and body language, also how to share, and respect the alpha pair.

ALL GROWN UP

Fast forward to when our wolf friends are about two to three years old. They're not teens anymore; *they're all grown up!* They're now **full-fledged members of the pack**, with all the strength and smarts they need to take on the world.

By this age, wolves have learned all the cool wolfy things that make them excellent pack members. They know how to hunt, howl in perfect harmony, and sneak up on their dinner without making a peep. Some of these adult wolves might decide to stay with their original pack, right where they grew up, the same way some people choose to live in their hometown with all their friends and family nearby. They know the neighborhood, have their buddies, and feel like part of a team.

But for some wolves, the call of the wild is *too strong to resist*. They might leave their pack to find

new lands and start their own families. It's a big, brave step! When a wolf leaves its pack, it's called **dispersing**. Dispersing wolves travel far and wide, crossing rivers, mountains, and valleys. They're true adventurers exploring new worlds, looking for the perfect new place to call home and maybe even a partner to share it with.

When wolves are around three to four years old, they're ready for one of their biggest steps: becoming parents and starting their own families. They begin looking for a partner at that age, and they'll

have a litter of pups together. The strongest and wisest parents of the pack become the alpha pair, ensuring pups are safe, teaching them how to hunt, and showing them all the best places to play and explore. They're like teachers and protectors all rolled into one.

Wolves in the wild usually live to be about 6 to 8 years old. But it's not common because life can be tricky with all its challenges. Some wolves, though, can get lucky and live longer, even up to 13 years, if they're good at hunting and staying safe.

Now, if a wolf lives in **captivity**, as in a sanctuary or zoo, it has humans to look after it. Since it doesn't

have to worry about finding food or staying away from danger, it can live even longer! These wolves might live up to 16 or 17 years old.

So, as the moon rises and the wolves howl, we see that life in the pack goes on. New leaders are born, new adventures begin, and wolves' wild, incredible life cycle continues.

FUR THE LOVE OF WOLVES!

WELL DONE, WOLF EXPERT!

Wow! What an incredible journey we've had exploring the wonderful world of wolves! From their amazing hunting skills to their powerful howls, from their tight-knit family bonds to their incredible senses, you've discovered all the fascinating things that make wolves such remarkable animals.

Think about all the fantastic things you now know! You've learned how wolf packs work together like a perfect team, how clever wolf parents teach their pups all about survival, and how different wolves have adapted to live everywhere, from icy Arctic tundra to scorching deserts. **Give yourselves a round of applause—you've earned it!**

Some wolves face challenges in the wild, but dedicated scientists and wildlife experts are working hard to protect these magnificent animals. By learning about wolves and sharing what you know, you're helping others understand just how special

they are. *Who knows?* Maybe someday you'll get to see wild wolves running free in their natural home!

Remember, every wolf has an amazing story, and now you know how to tell it. Whether you're explaining how Arctic wolves survive in the freezing north or sharing fun facts about how wolf pups learn to howl, you're now a true wolf expert!

Thank you for joining us on this wild adventure through the world of wolves. Now go out there and share your fantastic wolf knowledge with everyone you meet!

THANK YOU!

Thank you for reading this book and for allowing us to share our love for wolves with you!

If you've enjoyed this book, please let us know by leaving a rating and a brief review wherever you made your purchase! This helps us spread the word to other readers!

Thank you for your time, and have an awesome day!

For more information, please visit:
www.animalreads.com

© Copyright 2025 — All rights reserved Admore Publishing

ISBN: 978-3-96772-179-9

ISBN: 978-3-96772-180-5

ISBN: 978-3-96772-181-2

Animal Reads at www.animalreads.com

The content contained within this book may not be reproduced, duplicated, or transmitted without direct written permission from the author or the publisher.

Under no circumstances will any blame or legal responsibility be held against the publisher or author for any damages, reparation, or monetary loss due to the information contained within this book. Either directly or indirectly.

Published by Admore Publishing: Gotenstraße, Berlin, Germany

www.admorepublishing.com

www.ingramcontent.com/pod-product-compliance
Lightning Source LLC
LaVergne TN
LVHW021340080526
838202LV00004B/244